This volume first published 1974 by
Leslie Frewin Publishers Limited,
Five Goodwin's Court,
Saint Martin's Lane,
London WC2N 4LL, England.

Printed in Great Britain by
Biddles Ltd, Guildford, Surrey

Frontispiece photograph by Roloff Beny © 1973.

ISBN 0 85632 061 7

# THE COLLECTED POEMS OF SARAH CHURCHILL

## With Songs by Some of her Friends

LESLIE FREWIN of LONDON

# CONTENTS

# INTRODUCTION

This collection of poetry and songs contains the essence of my two previous volumes, *The Empty Spaces* and *The Unwanted Statue*.

The first was dedicated to my sister Diana, the second to my brother Randolph. Since they are no longer here, I am sure they will not mind in their absence my dedicating this volume of *Collected Poems* to my friends, some of whom have themselves written verses in the section *Songs By Some of My Friends*. It has not been possible to collect in this one book all those friends who write verse and music. But let me say to those who are not included: it is not that I have forgotten you, but time and tide and geography have not made it possible to reach you all just now. But since so many of you have enriched my life, those not represented are remembered with love and gratitude.

My present thanks are due to my publisher, Leslie Frewin, no mean poet in his own right; Charles Hamblett, author, journalist and poet; Patrick Desmond who has directed me in many plays and helped edit my work; Lobo Nocho, artist, singer and painter, who designed the jackets of my first two books of poetry. Acknowledged with gratitude, too, are Hal Shaper, poet, lyricist and composer, and Julia Lockwood, who, like her mother, never fails to decorate a theatre and who nowadays displays unexpected and welcome ventures into painting and verse. Anthony Montague Browne, for sixteen years my father's invaluable and trusted aide, has, I am glad to record, entrusted me with his first poem to be published. Villiers David, writer, painter and wit, I met during the war when I was for a short time closeted with him and a few others on a project. He enlightened the lunchtime breaks by modestly reading his own work to us and in turn inspired me by his challenge. And, from across the ocean, Alec Wilder, composer and poet, who listened to my burblings through the din of New York traffic with patience and fortitude and the sensitivity born of his own music. And, I am especially grateful, of course, to my sister, Mary Soames, who until I reminded her, had forgotten she had ever written poetry at all!

*London, 1974*                                      *Sarah Churchill*

# I
# LIVING

# A MATTER OF CHOICE

This is what I have chosen –
This moment bitter and free;
This is what I have chosen
From so much that was offered to me,
Life showered her costliest gifts
And a safe passage home, if need be,
But this is what I have chosen –
This moment so bitter . . .
And free.
Come, see what it is that I've chosen
Come, look on the dust that I see
Come, gape at the desert I've chosen
From all that was offered to me.
I bought these bright tears with a heart-break,
And they're all the jewels you'll see
Adorning this moment I've chosen
Dark moment so bitter . , .
But free

# ETERNITY

Eternity is life, when love has gone.
There is no sunset and no dawn –
Only the dead, monotonous grey
Of some interminable unending day.

# SKELETON

Don't pick at my bones,
Oh threadbare people,
Leave what is left
Alone
Well alone.
The marrow is still alive
And quick and keen,
Leave me alone.
Do not probe and pry
And dig too much
At what can never be seen.
What if I picked and probed
And scratched something
From off your bone?
Leave the skeleton that swings
From a beribboned pole
In a darkened sky . . .
Alone.

# BEYOND DESPAIR

I want to eat through this seedy seed of life,
These yearning, sorrowing hopes that lead to strife.

I want to see the heavens clear,
Undimmed by vastness, or obscured by fear.

I want to use these hands of mine
To hold and cherish whatever is.
I want to use my eyes to see –
My feet, to speed a million miles, if it should be
A sigh should want to meet an equal sigh.

For nature cannot so outrun herself,
That we, the casual passers-by, should sleep
While nature wreaks her havoc on us,
Telling us our time is done –
Then, when we wake, tell us, it is all undone
And we've to start again!

In my corner of the square, lies Nightmare,
And next to her, for closest kin, Futility
And next to her – Despair.

Preach me no doctrines of Chastity, Hope or Charity,
Preach me rather that the End is near.

I will confront the Gods
And make all preparations to be there.

# PASSAGE OF TIME

The years go slipping through my fingers
The days are long, the nights are cold
To what avail the dream still lingers
When the tale is never told.

Who sees a seed that never flowers
Who heeds a bell that's never rung.
Who knows of rain
But for the showers,
Of music, till the song is sung.

The years go slipping through my fingers
As water through a small child's grasp
Mocking the pent-up hope that lingers
Silent and barren in my clasp.

# ONLY THE YOUNG GROW OLD

Only the young despair!
Only the young are cold!
Only the young can cease to care!
Only the young grow old!

The years will mark the face,
And sorrow strain the heart,
But only the young can lose the race,
For the old no longer take part!

So here's to the young, who must lose,
And here's to the old, who have lost.
In youth or age there's little to choose,
And tears are the common cost.

For whether you sigh at the close of day,
Or sigh at the break of dawn,
There are tears for what you pray,
And tears for what has gone!

# TEA AT THE RITZ

The potted palm court,
The stucco world,
The genteel chairs
So worn.
The empty rooms,
The staring air
Of that octogenarian
Over there.

The tea will be weak
And not very hot
And the scones have had their day
But it's Sunday afternoon, my dear,
What else is there to do?
What else to say?
My God!
'What?'
I believe he's dead
'Who?'
That octogenarian
Over there.

# MORTALITY

You can get to the top of the hill
If you're young and tough and gay,
But take a coat and mind the chill,
For when you've reached
The top of the hill,
The sun may have slipped away.

The world will bend to a will
That's supple and strong as steel,
But after a life of an iron will
You'd better not look
For a sweet briar thrill,
For a dead heart cannot feel.

The butterfly on the hill,
The rose that blooms for a day,
The lark that sings on high,
You can have them all, if you will.

But a butterfly's sad on a pin,
And the rose is drab in a book,
And the lark just a bird
When his voice is still. . . .

And the trouble it takes,
And the time that goes
To capture desire
That must fade like the rose
The moment it comes to hand.

Leave the butterfly on the hill,
The rose to flourish and die,
The lark to finish its trill,
And your dearest desire – pass by.

# THOUGHTS AND MORE

Think no further than a thought's end.
To do so might contrive an end
That may not yet have found its meaning:

And to seal it now, may strangle it alive.

Where the thought ends – let it lie –
Whether it be for comfort or despair,
Leave it lying, with the other dead ends there.

It is not worse, than what is left for you –
When suddenly in flight, you stop and stare
And are gathered, garnished or abandoned.

You're no better off than that bright sentence or
    heady thought,
That hanged itself, somewhere, in the lifeless air.

Take your day with you to bed
And leave the thought that ends
As you must leave the dead.

And should a resurrection come?
Dear Friend, we'll talk of that anon.

# FOR FAME?

For Fame?
For the tinsel crown?
For the sugared word
Of a casual fool?
For the gaping crowd?
No. . . .

For the peace of mind,
For rest from thought,
For the good night's sleep
That has no dreams,
For mastery of Time that I must spend
To live life full and well,
And hurry to its end!

# THE UNWANTED STATUE

*A three dimensioned Christ*
*Cast aside*
*In an untended back garden.*

One Christ dying
Lies on its face
One Christ dead sleeps
With closed eyes
Though ligaments of one arm are torn and strained.

The third Christ lifts his body to the skies
With outstretched arms
The face bewildered, compassionate and pained.

The rust on the iron-green mould
Stains like old blood.
We creep around and bend to see again
The Jesus face that dies
But cannot for it lies
Face down into the ground.

We bend to see the face in sleep
We see and weep.
Then leave, turning our backs on the Christ
Arisen and alive
And talk of other things.

An old man walks on a traffic road
We stop and say, 'Good-day'

Then, for something else to say,
'By the way
Did you know James Joyce in his day?'
'No, I knew his father
That was enough.'
He goes his way.

He is a solicitor
Custodian of the Unwanted Christ
That lies among the grasses and the weeds
And the small animals that stroke the dying face
So close to the breathing ground.

*Here, an heroic concept*
*Of man's predicament lies*
*No need for any song*
*No need to moralise.*

***Eire, September 4, 1968***

# AUGUST 1933

Take me when I am young and true
When desires are many and fears are few
Take me when I am wild and strong
With a heart and throat that throbs with song
Take me when I am craving much
And sensitive to sight and touch
Spare me the horror of growing old
When my mind must be frail and my limbs so cold.

Spare me the greyness of middle age
Trapped with the rest in convention's cage
Take me while life is painfully sweet
While illusion reigns, while I'm incomplete
Take me when I most wish to live
While I still have something worthy to give.

When I am young and clear
Filled with the living breath
Take me, take me
Shadowy Death.

# A DEATH

Just twenty summers from the day of birth
You were killed
Death swooped down to earth and took you
Greedily seizing you in your prime.
Denying you your share of life
Stilling the longing ache for strife
That lit your soul
And urged you ever forward to the goal
All hopefully create
To soothe their human fears.

And now you're dead
And all the trials of those twenty years
That made you
Are gone too
Leaving an echo that we'll love yet dread
Till it, too, dies and we forget you.

*1933*

# YOUTH AND AGE

With wagging finger and shaking head
They came to me and said
Dream not so
Listen and learn from us, the wise, the aged
'Tis Youth's poor fancy
We know
We from whom youth has basely fled.

*With hardened hearts and lips they spoke*
*Calm cruel words that broke*
*All the dreams and thoughts I'd hoped*
*And I awoke*
*In bitterness, for it ever seems*
*That Age at Youth will mock and joke.*

They said
When we were young
We too had hopes, we sung
The glorious hymn of Youth
We too knew once the virtue Truth
And whilst through troubled veins
Our blood ran high and strong
We too cherishing our pains
In clamorous folly marched along.

But now we know it was illusion
A ceaseless rush, one mad confusion
Youth with all its painted magic

Was strangely empty, strangely tragic.
Thus dream no more
But rest with us upon the shore
Of age
Come not and trouble us
With dreams that we forgot.

Thus speak the old, their passion spent
And sit disconsolate and discontent
Upon an edge of life
Hearing the cries of distant strife
That they would drown
Remembering that it rung
In vain upon their ears
When they were young.

*February, 1933*

# A FLASH OF LIGHT

A flash of light:
Was it the sun?
Or was it reflection
Caught in a glass?
A splash of light
From the flash of a gun?
Or only the light
Of some midnight sun?
Was a curtain drawn back
In a darkened room,
Or a match struck
In the dark?
Or were forest fires leaping and reaching their mark?
Was it quicksilver dropped on the floor?
Or a pinpoint of light
From sound-shattered glass?
Or silver-tipped ripples of light
On deep cold water
Or shimmering grass?

What was it?
This flash,
This spark,
This fire,
This light?
What was
This dazzling spearpoint of light
In my night?

# NEW YEAR'S EVE

I crave and sigh for peace
For one brief pause, one moment's rest
Some soothing song to lull the heart
That pounds within my breast.

And yet if pain should cease
There was no ache, no throbbing smart
But confidence serene instead
Then would I know
That I was dead.

*1933*

# QUESTION AND ANSWER

*Q.* What do I dream of?

*A.* I am disembodied when I dream.
I think I dance on specks of light,
And in between
The pounding or the lapping foam
Of other seas.
I never think of home.
I am disembodied – I am free.
High above the storms I fly,
Or chase the lace-frilled edge of tides
That stretch their greedy fingers to ensnare me.

They never do.
In my dreams, I fly
Above and through
All storms
As a bird,
Offering no resistance to the wind.
Slips, on some eddying air drift through
And out, and on, and far beyond
The grasping hands that snatch at me.
A bird perhaps is nearest what I am,
The one whose instinct never lets it down,
Who sleeps in peace upon the storm's own **battling**
wind
And roar
And finds its earthly paradise
Upon some sunny shore.

But not for long –
Sun, blue skies, dates, palms, colour, grape,
Fade before the heartbeat and the call
That is in me,
And once again the bird is on the wing –
Into the unknown air I spring –
Away from sunlit shore,
Back on a stormlit sky
Toward a Northern clime.
No-one shall have me –
Child of earth's own turmoil,
There is no rest for such as me.
But my songs are for the singing
And my heart is for the free.

# TIME IS A CURVE

Look into the bright, bright sun:
Be not afraid
The stinging dark, the tears,
The ever-growing pall that comes, these
The burning light must bring.
Look, till colour has ebbed away:
And in the gentle tear-filled grey
Of equal ray
And shadow,
Look how the tears that splash about your cheeks
      and hands
Fluorescent glow,
And are among
The scattering of stars
The bursting skies have flung
When other dawns were young.

Look Onwards or Past
For now the eye can see;
And you may catch
Glints of yester moons
Still riding flinty seas,
And then beyond – there – there again
Is suddenly,
The glory of the sun
Hitting on burnished gods of gold,
Striking off daggers of light
To blind your eyes, even
A million years ago – a million years . . . ago?

30

Time the Teaser, the Wayward,
The Loser, the Lingerer,
The Usurper, the Murderer
The Curve –
Lies in this glimpse.
A child's marble – a lover's ring,
A man's nerve, a cynic's plaything.
A wise man's memory,
A prophet's sigh,
A Saint's eternal homage to the blinding light
    of the unveiling sky.

# POINT OF BEGINNING

As narrow is the end,
As wide the view,
Diamond shaped, the pattern
And the start begins with you.
From point nothing where you are
Until the widest you expand
And then perspective lends an icy hand.
The lines diminish to a narrow pointed end
Which is where you stand
No matter what your point of view.

# IL N'Y A QUE LA VIE

*J'ai tort!*
*Mais tout le même*
*La soirée dorée*
*Arrive quand même*

*J'ai raison!*
*Mais tout d'un coup*
*Je voie à la porte*
*Mon desespoir*
*Habillé bien*
*En soie et noir*

*Et je me dis*
*Ce n'est rien*
*On peut avoir tort*
*Il n'y a que la Vie*
*Et la Vie est si près de la Mort.*

# 1969

You talk of Perfidious Albion?
What about the other races
What about their smiling faces
Concealing under smiles
Half-truths, half-lies?
With half-shut, half-opened eyes
The handshake loses grip
The homely words of greeting slip
Into the meaningless of their faces.

And truths and lies
Disappear once more
Into the void of empty beings
That leave no memories of laughter or of tears.
Even a hamster trotting on fresh fallen snow
Leaves traces
But not your smile
Or guile.

Move from this temporary sorrow
Quickly
Forget the sudden feeling
Of gratefulness for shielding
This heart-worn heart

Since there was no real beginning
There'll be no need to part.

# EXIT

Where should I go
But to my grave discreetly?
Sober and quiet and most of all
In sombre dress announcing my defeat
Then there will be flowers!
And people mourning at my bier
Saying 'She was really quite a dear'
Because, like them,
I will have lost my meaning
And all of yesteryear!

# WHY?

Should it be necessary to say
What we are?
Why words
When looks can kill?
Why cultivate the gentle arts?
What price music,
Or the unsung song
When so many songs are sung?

Why take up your pen,
Why care
Or tear your heart again?

*Why?*

If I knew why
I would lay down my pen
And die.

# I WOULD LIKE

*I would like –*
*What would I like?*

I would like to draw
The curtain of the night
Across my mind
And drop
Into velvet darkness
And *STOP*
Free of jar and blare,
And the deafness of the human stare.

# 1933

Not of your race?
Then what am I?
Perhaps some long forgotten
Poet's sigh
A tear, unnoticed, that rolled down a cheek
And through the weight of years still tries to speak?

# DUST

There are no words
But this feeling
Is as old as Time
And faces longer than known Time
Tell about the heartbreak of their lives
And one is at once
Alone
And yet together
With humanity.

They look away
They must
Counting particles
Of dust is not inspiring
Work must go on.

There are no words
The best is silence,
With the Immortal Guest.

# WHERE DO I GO WHEN IT RAINS?

Out into the bitter wind and sea
Pushing out my frail slip of a ship
I bend to the high wind of despair
And clinging on with all my might
I sail out and plunge into the stormy night.

What good would a lighted, ordered room do me?
And people sitting chatting by the fire
Even a glance of compassion becomes a sting
That whips my hurt into a shameful thing
No – I go out into the wild wild seas
Where there are wild men clinging to the tiller of their ships.

Adrift, I am helped aboard,
I speak to the Captain above the raging storm. **He** does **not**
    hear me.
I make signs of word communication
But his eyes are on the raging seas ahead
And he does not see me
I turn my back to the icy wind
Like a skeleton the ship rises in silhouette
Bits of sail whip tattered and torn about the mast
Here there are no soft banners to signal
'Everything will come all right'
The only thought that comes to mind
'Will the ship last one more night?'
I open my mouth to call and plead
But the crashing music of despair

40

Shuts it
Edging my way along
The sliding slipping decks
I fight my way perilously back to the bridge
To a silent and wild Captain on the bridge
Clinging on with all his might
As his ship pitches and tosses
And the storm rages to its height
But wild men are sometimes strong
So I grit my teeth and hang on tight.
Presently I will slip back into my slip of a ship
And head it towards a calmer sea, towards the shore
Then drag it up the shingle and dump it on the beach
And wonder how a little thing dared go so far!
I'll breathe the air and look back at the forbidding sea
And pray that wild men never leave the tiller of their ships
And raise a soft-spun banner as a sign
That I have got to shore . . .

*Then I will face the task of going home*
*Everything will be there, as before*
*No need to tell them a thing*
*And worry them, and spoil*
*All they have wrought with tender care*
*Too proud to cry in shallow seas*
*Too late*
*When guts start melting with despair.*

# LONELINESS

The circumference of loneliness
Is the inability to communicate
The inexplicableness of grief
When ordinary ways of safety and conventions
Seem yet a further barrier to expression.

Being 'happily alone' is safe
The noises of the world go on
Gently
People talk – shoes squeak
Blinds flap softly in the breeze
Outside there is an illusion that
Life is
And goes on
China rattles, even breaks
People run upstairs
A door bell rings
None of these pertain to you
You recognise them, absorb them, warm to them
But lose them too
As you dwell within yourself.

The noises will continue forever
You are not afraid
You do not feel left out
Life is your pageant when you are happily alone
A bazaar your eye can drift over
Choosing this or that

And then not choosing
As you dwell peacefully within
The house of yourself.

But loneliness?
That is different.
Loneliness
Is the limit of your eye and feeling
Loneliness is beyond safe horizons
Loneliness is where there is no explanation
No reason ever asked
Loneliness is the stars
The falling spaces
Loneliness is a void on which
You must force dimensions
If you are to survive the endless years
The monotony of nature
Its smug satisfaction
Of death in life and life in death

# II
# LOVE

# LOVE

Spun glass and gold,
Fragile as a twist of thread –
Invisible almost in the sun
Like a darting dragonfly,
Now here, now there, now gone.

# THE ROOF

I'm detached, I'm aloof
I'm on top of the roof!
The world smoulders in smoke
But I'm breathing air
I'm free, I could choke
Do you hear me down there?
I'm chasing the moon and the stars up above
I'm mocking them, teasing them
For I'm not in love!
Yet I'll be appeasing them
Only too soon, I'm falling, I fear,
For you? O no dear!
Still, I'm not so aloof, and if the truth
Would be known,
I'm tired of being up here all alone.

# TOWN AND COUNTRY LOVES

When we two meet
In some noisy London street
And the heavy smoke-grimed air
Is red with the harsh electric glare
Of a million blatant signs.
When chimney pots seem lines
Of dwarfed and crooked little men
And thoughts likewise are twisted – then
My heart begins to beat
To the rhythmic sound of pattering feet
That hurry and surge around us two
And I feel lit with a quickening glow
And gaily for an hour or so
I am in love with you . . .

But with you, O country love!
'Tis different. Here the sky is blue above
And there's silence so profound
That one can hear the dew
Drip softly from the trees
That sway and tremble in the morning breeze.
And when we walk on grassy ground,
Soft and tender beneath our feet,
What I wonder could be more sweet
Than by your side to admire the view
Your horse, your tweed, it matters not
London's dusty thrill forgot
In my contentment to be with you.

*1932*

# MOONGAZER

I saw the moon as a jewel of delight
For all to wear who love the night
And stood and gazed with widening eyes
At the blue opaqueness of starry skies,
Innocently thinking you were wondering too
Instead
'I'm not feeling romantic,' you said!

'Fool, hateful fool,' I cried
And anger like a searing flame
Flared for a moment, then crumpling died
To sudden blushing shame
Of tears I would not shed.
Speechless, from your mocking voice I fled.

*1932*

# LULLABY

Let him go
Let him go
Let him go,
Let the pain die
Stifle that sigh
Dry up those tears
For they show
The easy way to your foolish heart.

'But I loved him so.'

No, no, no,
Let him go, let him go,
Let him go.

'But why, why, why?'

There is no why
If he cared
He would turn his feet
At the end of the street . . .
How foolish to stare
Down an empty street!
The patter of feet
You hear, are your own;
Look around – see –
You are alone.
Only the sharp-edged buildings show,
Let him go, let him go,
Let him go!

# SONG OF THE SIREN

Let the boat idle in the harbour, sailor
Creaking gently on the lapping tide
There'll be other days to go sea-riding, sailor,
Let the boat idle and come with me.
Today is for the flowering scented lanes
With blossoms hiding
In profusion under the green **protective** leaves.

Today's no day for the sea, **sailor**
She's content to be at rest
As peacefully as the ships upon her breast.
Why, look!
She scarcely breathes,
But lies lazy as a lake
Undisturbed by bird or sailboat wake

Come with me, sailor
I know a hollow and a shallow stream
That we can sit beside and dream,
And if suddenly you should stir
And wish for raging storm and tempest,
Lay your head upon my breast
And listen to the swelling tide
That is in me;
Oh, sailor
Stay.
On land,
I am your sea.

# PLATONIC LOVE

Is there such a thing as platonic
Love?
I would say so.
And be and feel
Something of a god
To love you, as dearly as I do,
And still let go . . .
Feel you
Trickle through and by me
As cold clear water
Through my cupped hand
Would do.

Yes—there is platonic Love
And Friendship without end.
But I am not a god
Nor would I be!
And so –
Roll on, old world of makeshift mortal Love,
What price Eternity!
If you
Can never love me . . .

# IF WE HAD NEVER MET!

I could write shining lines
About the wintry skies!
And paint in coloured verse
The silhouettes of trees that rise
So hauntingly detached and clear,
If we had never met! As 'tis, I curse!
My heart is jealous and confines
All thought to wishing you were near.

# ROSES IN THE DARK

Once more I hear the music of the lark
Piping clear and shrill,
Oh, there it is again, my heart,
Trilling as sweetly still.

Once more I hear the softness of your voice
Above the thunder of despair,
Confusion, doubt and folly pass,
Leaving our love still fair.

For ever ever will I hear the lark,
And see you gathering roses in the dark.

# SOMETIMES AT NIGHT

Sometimes at night
When the moon shines through,
I lie in my bed
And think of you.
And the shadows of trees
Sway on the wall,
And I say to myself,
I feel nothing at all;
Nothing, nothing,
Nothing at all!
And yet at night
When the moon shines through,
I lie in my bed!
And think of you!
I think no word,
No thought, no sigh.
As dead men stare
With unblinking eye,
I stare at the shadows on the wall
That swing, and sway, and rise and fall —
And feel nothing, nothing,
Nothing at all!
Only the moon keeps shining through,
Only, I can't stop thinking of you.
Joy and pain, I know, will end,
But how can nothing ever end?
And the shadows sway
On the bedroom wall
And I lie in bed
And I think of you

And the moonlight bright
Keeps shining through.
Oh, someone, someone,
Hear me call!
Stop the moonlight shining through,
Stop the shadows upon the wall,
Stop me feeling nothing at all!

# THE WEARY HEART

I could be happy, if my heart could rest
As lightly as my head, upon your breast;
I.could be happy, if my heart could say
'This is my journey's end; here will I stay'
I could be happy, if indeed I knew
Whatever stormy path, the last, was you;
This would be happiness if this were so,
And all of heaven, that I'd ask to know.

For this is the dream all humans dream.
There is no heart so base
That does not in the darkness grope
Towards this fevered and elusive hope.
The smile upon this face,
These eyes that shine so bright,
No love so poor it does not dream
'Tis not a mirage of the night,
It is at last the harbour's beam.

Dearest and newest of my fitful dreams
Yonder, the harbour gleams
Or so it seems!
Then why does my heart so tensely rest,
Why does my head but pause upon your breast,
For I could be happy, this at least I know,
If here my heart could rest, and never go!

# SONG

No place is home any more,
No pillow familiar to my head,
For the words that my loved one spoke are dust
And his face is strange and dead.

Oh, where can I find me a couch
To lay my limbs upon;
Oh, where can I find me a shroud
For a love that's dead and gone?

I'll turn my face to the wall
And let all the world be told
That the chill of the tomb is warm
To the chill of Love grown cold!

# 45th STREET NEW YORK CITY

To think that I should walk around the block with you
And find Eternity – and Tomorrow too,
And dreams I thought had died or were not true;
Walking with your pale courage
And the lemon-scented essence of my will
That I had packed away
A whole life-long century for some other day!

Was there traffic?
Or did they stop it?
And what about the people?
Did they stare?
I would have
If I'd been there,
Watching us
Walking around the block
Without an earthly hope in view.
And yet your arm across my shoulder
Your barest touch
Was such
That my mind, distracted for a moment
From disastrous things,
Found suddenly again that everything was there.

My friends, steady and true,
Surety of purpose and of will
And gentleness again,
Like water playing round a mill,
Still indefinite, like an echo
From some far-off land

That in a childhood dream I knew...
Purity too crossed my mind
Like a shaft of light that shines across a room
When someone lifts the blind.

I found speech again,
And words that for a million years
I had not dared to utter
Stumbled in certain force from out of me.
Shamelessly I clung to you,
Oblivious for a moment
(Or was it two?)
Until I realised in my dizzy mind,
Reeling with happiness sky-high,
That all we did
Was walk around the block — and say goodbye!

# A FRIEND

A friend is someone neither to be leant on
Nor lent.
Lightly – that is.
Purer than 'Love' itself,
For, so much of 'Love' we know
Is Pride –
So much of Friendship – Love.

In 'Love', you ask –
No: demand the sky!
And storm at Time, in fear;
Knowing
That given Time
Your love may whittle down
And leave you with a heap of bones
And 'feet of clay'
That you must treasure fondly
And call Yesterday.

So much for 'Love'
Now for a Friend . . .

Hands are as important as in 'Love'
Yet somehow different.
The same skin and bones
And yet the very feel of them is different.
Friends exchange their hands.
Neither takes – yet both can give
And through some mystic side to Love

You both can part – and Live!
In 'Love', you would most surely die!
What is this mystic gift?
Even the growth of it
Is as mysterious as Love itself.
I am a woman, and would have you love me,
Now, now! and arrogantly say
That I will gladly die when the end
Comes
And come it will,
And yet, to really love you
And have you love me truly to the end,
It seems I must deny our 'Love'
To call you Friend.

# TIME OUT FROM GRIEF

You cannot alter what my heart is saying;
You cannot change its song.
Transpose it to a key more kind
My heart will know you're wrong.
But do not falter
From this game we're playing
Like foolish things it's brief,
But in its foolishness I find
Time out from grief.

# WHERE NO WORDS ARE . . .

I have talked much in my time,
Written much, too.
Let fly, like long-imprisoned birds,
My giddy thoughts.
I have dressed them up in rhyme,
Or sent them out boldly
Scarce concealed in prose,
To wander as wanton women,
Provocatively, in revealing clothes.
I've scarce had a thought but to my pen it's flown,
Or from my lips has fallen idly
As petals from a flower that's blown.

And yet, of you
I cannot write.
Round you who were the core of Spring,
Silence, like night,
Lets fall a velvet cloak.
Where no words are
What can my words avail?
Echoes will ring,
And memories glimmer pale,
As stars long dead
Still shaft their light of beauty on the world,
But speech has fled.

A flag that once flew gaily
Is now forever furled.

# MY HEART'S A SECRET PLACE

I've locked you in my secret heart,
And not a soul shall ever know
How hard it knocks against my breast,
Or how I love you so.

I'll leave you in your lonely splendour,
No foolish thought shall stir you there.
My wildest hope can only be
That I may always care.

The world may call me cold of heart,
And mock the pallor of my face,
But since your eyes have smiled at me –
My heart's a secret place.

# LOVE IS IN HYDE PARK

*for Mario Soldati*

In Hyde Park
Lovers don't hide
Thinkers stroll
And dreamers wander
Side by side.
In Hyde Park
Lovers lie and lie
Entwined upon the grass
Visible and yet unseen
By the others strolling by
Beneath the leafy green.

In Hyde Park,
Though no wall or tree may hide,
Lovers live their lives apart,
Locked in the privacy of the human heart.

In Hyde Park
Lovers lie
And lie;
O Lovers, lovers
Clasp the moment to your breasts
And you the others passing by
Turn away the peering eye
Leave them loving on the grass
Love – like Summer
All too soon must pass.

# TO R.B.

O yes, I care!
And that is something to be glad about,
For when you care
You cannot help
But leave about
A smattering of caring,
That even strangers
Knowing nothing of your love
Can somehow share;
And in the mid-day hustle of it all –
Recall
As they climb aboard a crowded bus
A golden day they knew,
And remembering – know – that they too
Have something
To be glad about.

O yes, I care –
Though if you ask me to define
This moment
And – precisely what it is I feel
Perhaps for once
I'd let it linger in the empty air.

I walk through marble halls,
A stranger takes my hand
And echoes fill the sounding halls,
With hurrying footsteps that are not
My own –
And yet – I know
I am alone.

O yes, I care
And though I run the golden fields
And touch the free and crystal sky
And though I live and move and breathe
I cannot tell you what I feel,
Or even why.
Sufficient I suppose to let the pulse beat as it does,
Now fast – now slow.
And love the sunlight on the sand
I dig my toes in.

O yes, I care.
For when I think
Of shimmering water – close
To reeds sky-high!
Sentinels of care
Pushing their sixteen inches high
Into the air –
Swaying and bending
To the wind
But painting – ne'er the less –
A deathless moment, in an evening sky.

O – yes –
Remembering all of this
I care.
But why? . . .
I tell you
I do not know
Just why.

An unaccustomed silence,
From the stars shines down.
So that perhaps is why,
Although I care,
I am suspended in mid-air:
Breathing with caution,
Wary of despair.
So let
This mist of undefined unspoken things
Envelop us
And fill our silence
With tales and legends;
For I would rather hear
Of ancient classic loves that were
Than turn around
And build again
Another castle in the air

**Rome, 1955**

# INTERVIEW

Reporter: *'Why did you climb it?'*
    Man: 'Well – the mountain was there.'
Reporter: *'I see – How did you dare do it?'*
    Man: 'Well – the dream of it was there.'
Reporter: *'I see – Why did you fall in love?'*
    Man: 'Well – she happened to be there.'
Reporter: *'But surely –'*
    Man: 'NO – never – surely –
           Just – painfully –
           Aware.'

# 1968

Walk away from doom
Cling not to what does not exist
Search for the night-scented stock that can bloom
In spite of your despair.

Lift that heart of yours
Look at beauty
Remember smiles
Turn your back on gloom
Remember always
The pale night-scented stock
That still can bloom
Walk on, walk away from your despair.

# A KIND OF PEACE

I will take my sorrow and twist it
Into a bright, bright thing
I will take my sorrow and make it
Sing
I will take my tears
And twirl them into chandeliers
And after I have done that
And everything
I will take my love to my heart
Empty and bare
And for a moment
We will both
Sleep peacefully there.

# QUARREL – 1932

I know not what it is with you
We are together
And we only argue
Purposely it seems you take a different view
And how I hate you
Yet, most annoying, when we are apart
I sometimes miss you
It's all too plain
I yearn to argue everything again
Right from the bitter start.

# OUR SPRING

So green was the green leaf
This year
So sweet our tender grief
This time there was no fear
To tear my heart out
On the edge of bliss
And mock the ending of our kiss.
*I never heard the cuckoo's warning cry*
*I never thought that this green Spring*
*Would die!*

For never, never was there any Spring
As our Spring!
Winter was dead, and sorrow spent
My heart slow learning
Found content
No feverish thing
Our Spring
But gentle, deep and dear.

*Oh, darling, take my hand,*
*Help me to understand*
*The winter that I see is drawing near.*

# SONG

I lay in your arms
Close to your heart
And we were the ends
Of the world apart.

Our hands did not touch
To say goodbye
And we were as near
As tears to a sigh.

# COME LIVE WITH ME

'Come live with me
And be my love
And we will great displeasure show
For all the littleness of life
And that pale vampire, woe!

We'll live within a moment's pause
Transfix each other's sigh
And browse about each other's minds
Till death itself pass by.

Seek your oblivion in a greying west
Where placid sea meets placid sky
I'll climb some lonely mountain's crest
And catch your eye!'

# INSTANTANEOUS DEATH

I will die of course
If you do not love me
But it will be a quick clean death
It will be all the stab of Springtime joy
And love when it was young
And walked triumphantly across the room
Knowing no defeat
*There was no thought of shame*
*No need to phrase, rephrase, and paraphrase a simple thing.*

*No need for lowered lids and hidden eyes*
*No need for undecided pauses, pointing up desire*
*No need, no need to cloak oneself in lies.*

It will be death I know
But not a sickly one
Of moribund excuses
It will be sharp and it will sting
Like ice cold water
It will be steel, it will be fire
It will be –
A sharp intake of breath
The day you tell me
No
I'll die a pure and instantaneous death.

# PROMISE

Darling
While you are away
I promise to be good and gay
I'll hold my head high in the street
And go my way with dancing feet
And when I work I'll do my best
And when I sleep I'll sleep to rest
And should you be away a year
This heart of mine will know no fear
And as to grieve it would not dare
Since your heart too is sheltered there.

I must not tell
But by my face
They'll know that heaven is an earthly place.

# THE BREAK

The silent night crawls by
Clocks in their towers
Drag the minutes
Into hours
Hours of emptiness that lie
Dead and cold upon my heart.
Round and round my aching brain
Thoughts
Like gnawing rats in pain
Tear all that's left
Apart.

Clocks in their towers
Strike the hours
And, one by one
The words I've said
Move uneasily about my bed.
I toss, I turn, I sigh
I think I sleep, but wake to cry
This time wordless to the silent sky
'What else could I have done?
What else, my love, have said?'

# ALONE

*All day long*
*It is with me*
*Sad, sad, song*
*Within me.*

A mournful melody
From some distant sea
Is the song of memory
A shadow in the sunlight
A purple fear that haunts the moonlight
A leaden weight that smothers sleep
*And I have wept till I have no more*
*Tears to weep.*

I implored the gods in vain
To lift this ache, to ease this pain –
But ever-ringing in my brain
Must I hear the cold refrain
Of memory, that chills me to the bone.
For now that you have gone, I am so desperately
Alone.

# APRIL

*What is it to love me?*
Know the worst
At any moment
The tanks will burst
And lightning strike the sky
And thunderous rumblings
From the mountains roar
And the lights go out.

Nibble at me,
And I will say
*'Kill me'*.

Love me
And I will find a way.

*1968*

# FOR MY MOTHER

So you are home! I'm so glad I could sing
That hills and streams with my singing would ring.

Home without you was a lamp without light
A flower without scent, a moonless night
I counted the days as they slowly slipped by
Like leaves off a tree, that are finished and die
Each withered brown leaf that dropped from the tree
Drew you steadfastly faithfully nearer to me.

*November, 1931*

# THE WAY TO SAY NO

'Twas my mama who taught me how
The elegance I wear
Could lead me to the state I'm in
But then her lessons stopped just there
Just exactly where, my love,
I need her counsel now.

She would say
I have no doubt
'Turn away
My dear
Conventions you must never flout
Although your heart
Beats true
But nice young ladies
Never fall
Quite like you
Beyond recall
So gather up your glove, my dear.
And shield that look of love, my dear
For nice young ladies
Never should
Suggest they'd love
Like others would
For nice young ladies
Never fall
Without a thought
Beyond recall!'

My eyes I shielded
My wit I wielded
And you have often sworn
The graces that you most admire
By me so well are worn
Well, 'twas my mama that you did praise
When with your golden gift of phrase
My cheeks you set aflame
And now that they are pale and white
And now that you don't sleep at night
It is not me that you should blame
For 'twas mama, my dearest love,
Who taught me not to leave my glove
And how to trail a backward glance
And learn that virtue and romance
My love
Should not be left to chance.

# THE ANSWER IS NO

Dear, dearest . . .
*No!*
Your name will never more
Appear
Upon a sheet of paper
That pressed within an envelope
Addressed
Precise and clear
Would in good time
Slip through the post box of your door.
*Now, never more, my dear.*

How can I write
Who only wrote to tell
All of my heartbeats of a day?
How could I ever use my pen
To say
The weather is chilly and
The sky is grey?

*Silence for a million years is better*
*Than one false, gay letter*
*Written casually to one*
*To whom I used to say*
*(Was it but yesterday?)*
*Dear, dearest . . .*
*No. . .*

The Postman's bag is lighter
And as he goes his way
He'll shift his bag and mutter
'I'm a lucky blighter –
Love's grown cold today.'

# III

# FIVE POEMS IN MEMORY
# OF HENRY AUDLEY

# ONE

Newer dust
Upon this place
Is shed.
We stand and see
And hold, and
Never cry again.
Under the pepper and the fir
He lies,
And the mountain at his feet
Waits the eternal
Sunrise.

*British Naval Cemetery*
*Malaga, July 1963*

# TWO

Speak the loved one's name softly,
Caress it with a sigh,
Let it linger in the air,
Let breezes
Carry it on high
To mountain tops
That snow in Summer
To falling streams
That seek their meadowed fields;
Let earth accept his name
And make it part
Of all her natural song.
Grasses
That rustle as the wind steals by
Tell, O tell his name
To every living and inanimate thing
So as I wander by
I will not know
Whose sigh
Whispers his name,
The earth – or I.

Tell of the beauty of a soul
That loved red earth
And dancing olive trees;
O dancing olive trees
Dance on for me,
Let not this sorrow blind my eye
To beauty he could see;
Let blessed birds fly

Wheel, soar and
Chatter to their eaves;
Tell of his name
All sounds of earth
That even when I sleep
My night thoughts
Sing his name.

*Marbella, August 1963*

# THREE

The first light of dawn
Calls me from my sleep
And tells me, before
I have a chance to thank a god
for momentary peace,
There is but once again
The endless barren plain.

To remember – yet not too much
Or I would not go on.
Gird on your armour
And mould a splendid calm upon your face
That can regard beauty dispassionately,
A foggy mist-dimmed eye
Could surely never see
The way the sunlight dappled on
A small and dingy street
Making it heaven, for him and me.

Gird up the loins
Make not too brave a face
But to yourself.
Whisper to the mirror
He is gone –
As with meticulous care
You armour you, against the natural stare
Of people.

Look back – but not too much.
Sunlight dapples still
Yet – dare I face it
Once again?
Too dispassionate, I would be
To say the sunlight shines as well today
As in the summer day we knew
In nineteen-sixty-three.

Time heals, they say.
I tell you – it just
Leavens you, to dust;
By corrosion or a mildewed way.
On and on we go
Small inch of earth and time
We tread
And, beggars for our fear,
Half of us wish that we were dead
The other,
That we could reappear.

Time heals?
No, memory is a limb
That falters in the end –
The loved one slips away
Free – free –
I pray.

*Marbella, August 1963*

# FOUR

To have
To hold
To feel it in your grasp,
And watch it slip away
As any other day.

Will I retain
Moments that we knew –
Can I, can I?
Through thunderclouds of grief
Will I hold on to beauty
And the image that he sought for
All his life –
However brief ?
Will my eye
My mind,
Doctor and change a theme he had
Or will I, when the silence comes
And others have forgotten,
Remember beauty as he saw and loved it?
And peace we knew
Too far from life
Too close to death,
So that minutes were an hour
An inch, too far apart.
Will my mind remember
The present of our love?

The secret that we shared
Two stricken souls
Meeting at last,
In an agreement of the heart?
Will I hold on
Or will I change
And become
Some dusty moth?
A derelict
Forever lost —
And lose within my heart
The unconditioned love he gave to me
To be, while I had life,
Unconditionally free.

*Marbella, August 1963*

# FIVE

Who could have known
That death was stalking
So close
Must I never again
Trust smiles?
Must I be wary
And walk
So close to my own virtue
And never trail my garment
In the dust?
Virtue is a thing
Of renown.
I have none
But walk alone to truth, loving and careful
Of my trust
Which is to live
And love again
Until this
Spirit drops into the ground
And turns to dust
To renew
That trust.

*Marbella, August 1963*

# IV

# SONGS WITH MUSIC

# I'VE LEFT YESTERDAY BEHIND ME

I've left yesterday behind me,
Yesterday was kind to me,
Hope I'll find a heart and mind to be,
Now that yesterday is gone.
I must find some new horizon,
Other stars to fix my eyes on,
Even while my heart within cries on,
Now that yesterday is gone.
For a stream flows on till it finds its sea,
And a star can shine though it's ceased to be,
And I am a part of this mystery
Which says, go on, go on.
So I will rise and leave my sorrow,
Seek and find some new tomorrow,
Though from the past I still can always borrow,
Although yesterday, yesterday,
Although yesterday has gone.

# THE HAPPY TIME

Oh, the happy time is the time between the times you
    should be there.
Oh, the happy time is the time it takes to get from
    here to there,
Like a ball thrown in the sky,
Or a swing poised in the air
Oh, the happy time is the time perhaps you're really
    not quite there.
Oh, the happy time is the time perhaps you're really
    not quite there.

# IMAGINE

Your lover has gone
He left without warning,
Your lover has gone,
He left you this morning.
What will you do now?
What will you say?
How should you spend the time of day?
Imagine, imagine,
That's what I'll do.
Imagine the things he'd say and he'd do.
And imagine that that's what he'd want me to do,
Imagine I will until it's true.
For life's a dream that is waiting to be
A dream that may some day come true.
So I shall hazard my own true guess,
And imagine the day that he'll say 'Yes'
Imagine I will,
Imagine I will,
Imagine I will until it's true.

# THE WILLOWS

Though I lose you,
I'll hold on to the dream,
So the willows will grow
And cherish the stream,
Though I lose you,
A bird in a tree
Will sing a new song
And remind me
Some days in the garden
The trees will be bare.
Those are the days
I know you're not there,
But though I lose you
I'll hold on to the dream,
So green grow the willows
That silver the stream.

# LOVE WILL HAVE ITS DAY

Thru' the chatter of the day
My mind will keep my heart at bay,
And never shall my heart find out
That my mind is full of doubt.
Heart shall rule though head be wise,
Heart must win or Juliet dies.
Heart can always spring surprise,
And love will have its day.
Heart must care when thoughts are wild.
Heart must dare till Fate's beguiled.
Heart must always be a child
And love will have its day.

# TROUBLE IS NO STRANGER HERE

What is the matter?
Why are you sad?
Tell me, tell me.
What is the matter?
It can't be that bad,
Tell me, tell me.
What is the matter?
Why are you blue?
Isn't there something that I could do?
What is the matter?
Oh, please have no fear.
Trouble is no stranger here.

# V
# SONGS WITHOUT MUSIC

# SONG

If I could recall my words,
As hunting ladies could
Their falcon birds,
I would! I would!

If I could deny their tale,
As painted ladies do
Their pallor frail,
I doubt I would!

How foolish, though, to let my words
Fly wildly as the falcon birds.
Falcon birds were never free,
Nor is the heart that sends these lines to thee!

# ENCHANTMENT

Come, leave this world of sound
Where even Love is valued at a price
Come where the purple night is bound
By chains of peace, and pallid stars that glisten
Come – bathe in the silence of this paradise
And listen . . .
Here the soothing song of streams
Is cooling balm to souls weighed down by fears,
Lie in the waters of forgotten dreams
Listen to the music as you float along
Let memory echo gently in your ears
Her Love song . . .
Taste if you will the fruits of passion
That hang like glowing jewels from spreading trees
Whose ever swaying shadows fashion
Heroic unborn dreams. But before dawn
Rises with the chilly morning breeze,
Be gone! . . .

*December 1932*

# PASSION

Music, music everywhere
Dripping, falling through the air
Piercing, soaking all my soul
Till it springs beyond control.

Soaring, soaring into space
Clasped and held in one embrace
Of colour ecstasy and sound
Then lowered gently to the ground

Silence, silence of the night
Till memory pale and ghostly white
Comes and batters at the door
And music fills my heart once more.

# TWILIGHT—*L'HEURE BLEUE*

*for Villiers David*

Here she comes again
Riding on delight –
Painted, panoplied and perfect,
Here she comes
On a summer's air of flight,
Here she comes again –
*L'heure bleue,*
The herald of the night.

Now are the buildings human,
Now are the people gods,
Now does the eye soften
As the day straightens her back
To touch the twilight
And prepare for night.

Now can I dream again,
Now can I sit and think
And dig into myself to find
Some joyous thought – on which to hang my mind!

Here she comes dancing
Ephemeral blue and slight,
Spreading her allure
Disarmingly,
On tree and neon light;
Here she comes
*L'heure bleue,*
Tenderfoot and gay
Fragilely entrancing,

As she drapes her cloak,
On the drab and grey –
Making everything she touches glisten
Oh, people, people, stop, look, listen
Before she slips into the night
And on her way!

**New York**

# LAKE OF GARDONNE

The ferryboat paddles across the lake
Churning the waters in its wake;
It's busy and quick and keen to go
On its short little journey to and fro.

I've seen no steamer more proudly float
Odd little, proud little, gay little boat,
Thinking the lake as big as a sea
It carries the people home to their tea.

It hurries and scurries four times a day;
It's serious business, it isn't at play
The Captain is proud, as so he should be
For who knows but Destiny's waiting for tea.

So hurry along, it won't wait for you
Any more than a great ocean liner would do
And it couldn't care less at the bother you make:
There's no other method of crossing the lake.

*January 1947*

# SONG

How like a man to say,
'See how my charm
Has made her smile today!'
And like a man,
When woman breaks her heart,
To turn away
And say he had no part!

# PALAZZO BONAPARTE, ROME

The huge lamp hangs
In the vast high hall,
Still, as a watching eye,
As a yellow, mellow, harvest moon
Hangs in a summer sky.

*1947*

# SILENCE

It's strange there's no way
To say
The simplest of things.
O – one can learn the art
Of expounding scintillatingly
The philosophy of the human heart.
But face to face
At a lonely hour
How is there a way
To say
The simplest of things?

There is a hand, there is a glance,
There is suddenly chatter that fills a room
But most of all there is silence
And someone who remembers –
To light a light
In a suddenly darkened room.

# SONG TO A SEASON

Spring!
Yet I have nothing new
To sing;
No more to say
Than that I love you
More and more
Each day.
And this sad song, dear heart,
Echoes more truly now
Than at the start!

Spring!
They say, new birth!
O mockery!
Merely the awakening
Of memory
Who stalks a naked earth,
Reviving flowers
But also pains,
And tears
I thought forgotten,
I find, with buds of May
Begotten
Once anew,
By April rains,
Falling from fickle skies
Of blue!

# COMPASSION

*For Sylvia Henley*


Compassion – a strange and lovely thing;
Not love exactly,
Yet an understanding
That leaves the stricken, proud and free
To wander – not completely
As might be –
Alone.
The void is momentarily filled,
The fear reined in
And willed to subjugation by the mind once more.
Despair's own pulse is stilled
By man's compassionate
Love dispassionate.

The unknown arms that rescue unknown soul
Can hold and seal the ebbing spirit force
That seeks in opposition to its birth
Extermination on its upward course . . .

So in the length and depth and breadth
Of the imagination's icy grip
Upon the soul
That pointless endless circulation
Might be our role.
It is the heart of Man that reaches out
Into the void –
To keep Man whole.

# LEAVE ME MY GRIEF

Leave me my grief,
Do not console me!
Leave me my woe,
Do not cajole me!
Force me not to smile.
Let me, dear friend,
Be sad awhile.
Let me please grieve,
Let my tears flow,
Forgive and believe
It will be better so.

I'll find some comfort in my pain,
Some reason in her barren arms
Than in the kindness of the truths you say.
I know that Spring will come again
With all the newness of her pale green charms.

Joy is brief.
I know, I know,
So let at least
My grief run slow!
Gaiety just now is out of place
As flaxen curls about an aged face.
Let winter stay.
Hold back the Spring.
Memory is evergreen,
And still as bright
As any green I've seen!

Let winter stay!
I like her sober dress.
Arrest the buds that press
Through the brown bosom of the earth.
Hold back the Spring!
Winter in her frozen heart
Holds everything!

# VALEDICTION

Goodbye, my dear,
Goodbye!
There still is much to say,
And yet
My tongue and pen, so wont to fly,
Have of a sudden both run dry.
Goodbye, my dear,
Goodbye!

I'll not forget.
Too near to heaven
Did everything comply!
But destiny is set
As are the stars on high.
Goodbye, my dear,
Goodbye!

# THEATRE FOR SALE

Never was anything so deserted
As this dimmed theatre
Now, when in passive greyness the remote
Morning is here
Daunting the wintry glitter of the pale
Half-lit chandelier.
Never was anything so deserted as this dimmed theatre
We stand upon the empty stage worn and bare
Already we are ghosts breathing the dusty air
Hearing in our souls the laughter and the tears . . .
Never was anything so deserted as this dimmed theatre.

# DAWN AT MALIBU

For the poor children who stay up late
There is the dawn
Birds do sing
And opal-blue and pure
The morning waits her turn
Unloved
But sure.

Hues rarely seen
Except by wanderers with time to burn
Drum out the night
With yellow flame
And shot-silk blues and greens
While in the sky the seagulls
Lazing on their wings
Scream
Piercing the ear
As they proclaim
'The dawn is here!'

Now night has come to Malibu
Now only do you hear
The hissing, pounding of the breakers
Cobalt blue.

On shore day sounds are gone

Once gain the wanderers
With time to burn
Move to the beaches
To await
The dawn's return.

# JANUARY **1932**

Oh what a state the world is in
We talk of nought but income tax and sin
Of Irish treaties and the water rate
Oh to what a low and bestial state
We've sunk!

Can no one see
The stars that ride the heavens free?
The sun, which never fails, and everyday
Rears his red head to warm men
On their way?

Does no one see the moon
Oh, blind, blind fools
Reflect her silver form in quivering pools
That lap your very door?
Are the songbirds heard no more?

Can nevermore the nightingale stir your hearts?
Or does it fail
To pierce the heavy armour you have wrought
Around your souls?
And have you fought so many fights
That you no longer hear
His shrill and passionate voice
So full and clear?

If this be so, then do I pity you
Your life, your work, and all the things you do

You have your incomes, rates and taxes
I have the moon
That wanes and waxes.
Look to your fickle stocks and shares
I have the song-birds, springtime airs
Keep, oh keep your serious faces
I'll take nature and her open-spaces.

# TO A ROSE

Rose, I envy you for you grow in glory
And from the first bursting of your dream
Until the end
When, in an extravagance of feeling
You throw your petals on the floor or grass,
You are the poet of all things that pass.

The delicacy of your youth
Pushing with steady purpose to full bloom
Must amaze the eye of god or cynic
And then the glory of your ripening
As, with a laugh, you spill yourself
With such a happiness of heart
That even your petals on the carpet lying
Are not a cause of mourning or of sighing

But a stab of conscience, a whiplash
Recalling to the mind and will
The tender, living beauty that surrounds us still.

# LAVENDER TIME

Lavender blue
Lavender mauve
Lavender grey
For you
Lavender glowing
Lavender rolled
In a hand that picks it
While it is growing
Lavender scenting
The afternoon air
Lavender painting the view
Lavender twixt
Finger and thumb
Lavender blue
For you.

Lavender mauve
Lavender blue
Invading the sky and the sea
And the view
Lavender at the end of the day
Melting away to a mist grey
To burst once more into the view
With a lavender shade
Of midnight blue
A lavender garden
Made by you.

# LEGERDEMAIN

Here it is!
Here! Look! . . . Catch it –
'What?' . . . Why this! . . .
This vacuum – this void – this
Nothing
*What d'you mean*
*'You cannot see it?'*
Here! Touch it!
I can
Here – feel its smooth lead surface.
See its shape?
Why, its like a ball
We could play cricket with it!
*What d'you mean*
*'You do not see it'*
I can feel it!
Here – take it!
*What d'you mean*
*'You do not understand'*
Look idiot! I hold it in my hand
*What d'you mean*
*'There's nothing there!'* . . .
Say no more . . .
I know what
I'll reduce it to a ping-pong ball
And swallow it
Like a conjuror
*What d'you mean*

*'Please don't' – that*
'Now you see it?'
Why the fuss?
I told you
There was nothing there.

# THE TIRED TOYS

Come now, come away
Leave what's undone
Come now little one
The story's done.

Come now, darling, Teddy won't cry
And floppy old doll won't really die
Come now, don't be sad
Only the day is through
And now that tonight's begun
A whole new world is waiting for you.

Come now, little one
Your toys are tired
If you go now
They won't be sad
They'll find their way
Into the cupboards where they belong
And sleep until it is day.

So come now, little one,
Come, come away.

# ON BEING ASKED
# WHEN I WAS COMING HOME

April will come
And April will go
With all its splendid show
And the daffodil
Will nod her head
And sway to the breeze that may sometimes blow
And the streams from the mountains
Released from the snow
Will babble again at will
So April will come
And April will go
And I
Will really try
To be home in time for tea.

So April will go her showery way
And May will take her place
And the buds will grow
And the flowers will be
And Spring will gently push her way
Through the old, dark earth of yesterday.

Gulls will swerve above the sea
As Summer strides her lazy way
And the corn and the hay grow high
And I?
Will make plans seriously
To be home in time for tea.

# TO ME

Hurry, hurry, hurry
Get on your way
Hurry, hurry, hurry
Now
The moment that's past
Cannot stay
The moment that will be
Will not be delayed
So hurry, hurry, hurry
Get yourself going,
And on your way.

Hurry, hurry, hurry
Get going
Now
Hurry, hurry, hurry
Fling everything into your case
Somehow.
That's right
There's really
No time to bow
Tear yourself free from yesterday
Don't delay.

Goodbye, goodbye, goodbye
I wish that I could stay

But I'll be late for
Tomorrow
If I stay
So forgive me
If I hurry, hurry, hurry
On my way.

# MONOLOGUE FOR ME

*Who would I write to, but 'me'*
*It has only happened to 'me'*
*So who should I tell but 'me'?*

Dear 'Me'
    I have secrets that you know
So it's easy to tell
What you already know
And you and 'me' can wander
Through the lanes together
And remember and remember.

There was a day (we never can tell)
When the green leaves tasting their first spring
Tenderly unfurled their leaves
As all newborns do
The sight broke both our hearts
And Springtime too

And then – where did we go?
Well, you *should* know
Isn't it strange that even between you and me
There are some roads we cannot go?

So that leaves
Just 'me'
I just lost my 'alter ego'
The road ahead is dry and clean

I'll buy a horse at the next store
And I'll wander to the desert
With a heart that's a store
Of what has been
What is more
I'll face what's in store . . .

# STATEMENT

A time to be me
A time to be myself
A time to be
*Me*
On the shelf.

# SALZBURG

I would be in England
Now that trees are bare
Robbed of their beauty I would be there.

I would be in England
Though by birds forsaken
And dawn no more by song is shaken.

I would be in England
Still at approaching death
To catch a sigh of her dying breath.

I would be in England
Now that autumnal calm
Soothes sore hearts with her funeral balm.

*September, 1932*

# ESCAPE FROM SELF

Why do I work and try?
Why do I worry and sigh?
Am I sure it's not all in vain?
Youth slips so easily by.

I work for the right to say
'Book me a seat for Rome'
My soul has need of its air
For oddly enough
I found it there.

I work for the right to say
'I've had enough of you all to-day —
I'm off!'
A spirit calls me home
I have need of Rome
*I wonder why in that foreign air*
*I do not feel a stranger there?*

Aeons ago
Did I lean my head
Against pillars raised
By hands long dead
And pray for some power
To carry me far away
To a land that's cool and green?
Was my spirit ever the same?
*Is pursuit always my aim?*

*Pursuit of a dream that eludes,*
*But lures.*

It's good, my friends
That I work and strive
For while there's any man
Left alive
It's the only cure
That cures.

# ROME AT CHRISTMAS

Snow scenes – but no snow
Lights glitter – but no lights glow
Letters posted to loves – but no loves show
An empty scene – bereft of snow.

*What to think? Where to go?*

Wander through the streets
And watch the gas balloons
That sway and flow

Answer shy-crept smiles
Of pride
As father walks with son
Fiesta-dressed
By his side

Or seek a church
Where majestic organ music and soft candles glow
And hear again the tale
Of joy and pain
And
Ultimately
Woe

Or seek a friend
And softly go
Out into the streets again

Letting the day
Go gently by
And watch the gas balloons that sway and flow
A Christmas night
Bereft of snow

*1964*

# HERALDS OF AUTUMN

The summer ends
And mellow light
Clings to the land

But slips at last
Reluctantly from sight
As loving finger tips in sleep must slip
From a beloved hand at night

Heralds of Autumn
In the brightest red
Have claimed already a leaf, a branch
On quite a dozen trees
That I can see
At the merest glance.

The sailor furls his sails
And puts away his boat
And birds start flying
Restlessly about
Irresolute it seems of purpose
Yet resolute on flight.

The sky leavens its hue
Dimming the blinding brightness of its former blue
And earth returns within herself again
Clasping her harvest of the golden and the new
That Summer left in her abandoned pleasure.

The squirrels peek and dart about
Storing away their treasure
The sea grows leaden and forbidding
And little birds cease dabbling
In the wake of waves
That splash the sandy sunlit shore
And the trees straighten themselves
In apprehension of the losing fight
As Summer ends.

# OCTOBER LEAF

We know too well your end
But for the moment
You are free to whirl and float
Up in the frosty autumn sky
Whirling and swooping and rising
Oh! drunken ascent
Wildly and supremely free
Bearing your message of ecstatic birth
You live your moment
Till crispen and bent
By the mocking wind you fall to earth
Satisfied, fulfilled, content
Oh! glorious descent.

*1932*

# AFTERMATH OF AUTUMN

Once coloured leaves
Lie sodden on the ground
And in the woods there's little sound
But the squelching gulp
Of one's feet upon the rotting pulp.

A lonely chilling breeze
Slips, unheard, unseen,
So easily between
The bare black branches of the trees
Gaunt fingers stretched towards the skies
Yearning for the pallid sun to rise.

# LIVING ALONE

Love the rain beating at your window or skylight
Hear how a house breathes
And notice how carpets have shifted a little
And pictures are leaning slightly askew
So you can put them right tomorrow.

Notice plants stretching out their tentacles
Gently at night
Wanting the light as you do
*Take your loneliness gently*
*And discover yet again what the lonely feel.*

The heart remains the same
Only the scenery is different
To what you hoped it would be

Catch up with sleep
And at the day's end
Make the pillow
Once more your friend . . .

# WHO CAN SAY?

Dying flowers leave fading scent
Falling leaves a coloured spell
But the moon is nearly spent
And memory as well.

Scent will die
Leaves must rot
And who's not known a moonless sky?
Oh, knowing this who can say
That even memory will not
In time like perfume fade away?

# VI

# WAR

# THE BOMBERS

Whenever I see them ride on high
Gleaming and proud in the morning sky
Or lying awake in bed at night
I hear them pass on their outward flight
I feel the mass of metal and guns
Delicate instruments, deadweight tons
Awkward, slow, bomb racks full
Straining away from the downward pull
Straining away from home and base
And I try to see the pilot's face.
I imagine a boy who's just left school
On whose quick-learnt skill and courage cool
Depend the lives of the men in his crew
And success of the job they have to do.
And something happens to me inside
That is deeper than grief, greater than pride
And though there is nothing I can say
I always look up as they go their way
And care and pray for every one,
And steel my heart to say,
    'Thy will be done'.

# ACW2* TO PILOT OFFICER

You're the ruddy blinking tops,
And good luck to you.
The best be where you go.
You're a straight-up proper smasher,
And I wish I'd told you so.
I'd heard more than I knew of you
And it hadn't all been good
But what I saw I liked a lot,
And I'd have told you, if I could.
I'd have told you, if I could,
But that's not how some things go;
That's not the way the cards were stacked,
And I was old enough to know.
But I know a 'smasher' when I see one,
As I know a 'son of', too!
And you're a 'no lark top-line winner'
And here's me telling you!

They say you're tough with women,
That your past with them – is mud,
That you're slick as hell in business
And of course it's in the blood! . . .
I found you gay and gentle
And quite a bit of fun,
And I suspect for all the women
You wished you had a son.
I found you unashamed to say
The things I know are true,
What wild horses wouldn't drag from me,
Came simply out of you.

154

Now I'm not saying you're all white,
But this I'm sure is true –
If there is any laughter – after,
We'll need some more like you!

You're the ruddy blinking tops,
And good luck to you.
The best be where you go.
You're a straight-up proper smasher,
And I wish I'd told you so.
I wish I'd told you so
That day you flew away,
But still, maybe, somehow, perhaps,
You knew it anyway!

*Aircraft Woman Second Class

# THE LAST MILE

Why is there dust
On your shoes,
Soldier?
Have you walked
So many a mile?
Where do you
Come from?
Where do you go,
Soldier?
Can't you smile?

Was there nothing
For you ever
That you can't
Dream of now?
Oh, come on, soldier
There is only, ever, only –
One last mile.

# 1943

The roll of glory reaps another name,
The mounting toll of grief goes on,
How gay and crowded is the house of fame,
How still the house from which you've gone.

It's all been said and felt before
But repetition does not ease the pain;
The battered heart that thought it felt no more
Learns it can break as bitterly again.

# R.A.F.

We will remember
We promise you
Whatever life may bring,
When river mists creep up and chill
And birds who love the summer wing
Their way to kinder skies
Fearing the wild December.
We will remember
We promise you.

We will remember
We promise you
If ever life should bring
Some measure to our dearest dream
And once again there should be Spring,
And we should live to know
A kindlier December.
We will remember
We promise you.
We will remember
We promise you
Whatever may unfold,
Be there but bitterness to reap
Still in despair we'll never lightly hold
Life which you loved and gave without a thought;
How could we cheapen
What was so dearly bought.
In Spring, in Summer and in December
We will remember
We will remember.

# THE REVOLUTIONARY'S LAST MOMENTS

Sure – I want to be a hero
Sure – I want to win the day
Sure – I want to see the flags
Flying free today.
And the glorious scudding clouds
Hurrying up to make the day
That's attendant on us now.

Sure – I like the bells a-ringing
Sure – I like the 'oohs' and 'aahs'
Shouldn't I?
For who's a-dying
While the gay flags go a-flying?

# THE EXECUTIONER

Save your last spit for the executioner;
Let him see your blazing eyes.
Walk with purpose more than mortal
To whatever lies.

Let him ponder till he dies
The burning question that he's left too late,
And shrug your spirit shoulders as he mumbles
'I was but an instrument of fate'.

# EIGHT A.M.

Too late for fear,
Too spent for tear,
The dawn drew up a dismal day,
The prisoner stepped into the light
Eternity claimed another day.

# OF LOVE AND WAR

That you were no longer there
I was reconciled to that
I still had heart to care
Each time I passed your flat
It was a pleasure to remember
You had known and loved a street
Some dingy, dirty street
Some dingy door
Celestial portal
Because upstairs there was your flat
That you were no longer there
I was reconciled to that.

Time had gone when dreaded pain
Could grip my heart reviving
All our foolishness again –
In spite of all my striving to forget
It was yet
A pleasure to remember.

Pain was gone I swear
I could pass our favourite place
And find it only sweet to care
Fearful only I'd forget your face
And wonder who was in your flat.

That you were no longer there
I was reconciled to that

But now the street has gone
Vanished forever is your door.

Not content with taking you
Life wantonly destroys
The places that we knew
Gone is our Church
Gone the corner store
Crumbled and shattered in the
Waste of war.

# REAPPRAISAL

Now is the time for stripping the spirit bare
Time for the burning of days ended and done
Idle solace of things that have been before
Rooted hope and fruitless desire are there.

*Let them go to the fire, with never a look behind*
*The world that was ours is a world that is ours no more.*

# AND YET

And the moss and grass grow round
The pedestals of statues
But fail to hide the scars.

Man's momentary vision of the future
And Man's eye, forever dimmed
Bars
Both the Present and the Past
And a child's wide eyed stare
At the uncomprehending world
Must fade at last.

Toys, smuts on noses mingle
With the shattered bones and hopes
Of Paradise on Earth.

And yet the sun still shines
Breeding grass and worms
Alike. And then, as if
In sudden revolt to herself
The Earth explodes again
Tearing apart
All it hoped to hold
And into the dustbin once again there goes
The eternal and the human heart.

# WAR CEMETERY

These are the tears of the Unknown
These are the days
Without sun
These are tears for what we do
And tears
For what we leave
Undone.

# VII

# REMEMBRANCE

# SEASIDE

I am a child in a seashell
Swaying forever in the sea
I love and live for.
The cool grit of sand strokes my feet
As I fly, barefoot along the beach
Apace with clouds and wind and spray
I see a seagull, lazing in the air,
I catch my breath and stop,
Motionless. And stare
Until it slide-slips into flight
And I slip into my seashell
And out of sight!

# CASUALTY

O the joy of cutting one's knee!
It hurts, it's a shock
Tears, screams, commotion
Iodine – Ouch!
And a change of frock.

The worst over one can review the scene,
Nanny, mother, cook
All came to see
And curse the rock
That had upset one's equilibrium

Loving arms restore
One's poise and glee
And really,
There's nothing to see –
O the joy of cutting one's knee!

# CHRISTMAS **1943**— CHEQUERS

There was a clink of glass
Friends grown thoughtful in the mellow gloom
Thought awhile on the years ahead
As the firelight leapt through the dim-lit room
And prayed that when those years were dead
And we'd reached the years that would come after
That revenge and hatred,
As our tears, would pass
And some of us would be left for laughter
After, after

# PENNIES TO SPARE

I had threepence worth of courage;
Not much for a long life,
And my purse was often low
From the needed and the needless strife.
And although, so often fearing
That my purse would soon be bare,
Miraculously,
At the moment needed,
I'd find one left to spare . . .
But then one day,
I plunged my hand in
And found my purse was bare.

Passive at last
And unresisting,
Not caring that my fight was lost,
I heard a small voice
Still persisting,
Whimper and be lost –
At last I've killed myself, I cried –
At last I needn't care;
At last I am beyond all pleading –
At last my purse is bare.

I closed my eyes and let the hubbub roar
Unheeding by . . .

. . . I stood transfixed,
My eyes downcast,
Immune at last from feeling,
From the scolding and cajoling
From ridicule and neglect,
From stupidity and warnings
We knew I would reject;
From the curious and indifferent,
From the barely ice-veiled threat,
From the ever easy reckoning
Of my merit or my debt –
Immune at last from caring,
From the prod, the poke, the stare,
Immune at last from all of caring –
Even from those who care,
Whose tearing eyes of pleading
I could no longer bear.
I stood and prayed for one last daring –
To hollow out my soul for hate
Beyond repairing.

I stood transfixed,
My eyes downcast –
When suddenly I saw
A penny gleaming on the floor.
I looked around –
But there was no-one there.
I picked it up – it wasn't mine,
It wasn't there before –
I showed it all around.

'Look – what I have found,' I cried,
'Is it yours, or yours?'
'Not mine or mine,'
They steadily replied:
'Better keep it – you may need it,
There's generally one to spare.'

I put it in my purse
And fingered it with care,
Whose? – when? – where?
I searched their faces,
But they shrugged their shoulders
And bestowed a smiling stare.

I stood transfixed, and pondered
On the penny I had found;
I stood, and found that I was once more caring,
And caring – held my ground.

# 1932

Why was I silent
When my heart was rent
By words I might have said
But now the moment o'er
Like dead or sighing ghosts
Some still unborn
They float through space
Forever gone.

# END OF THE LINE

Shut out the past
If you can
Close your sensitivity
To life
If you can
Forget the brilliant light
Of happier days.

Go for the shadow
Of mindless sleep
Drift into the tomb
Without a fight
Sink for a thousand days
Of forgetting
Heal the mind and soul
Of life's long ravaging
And pain

Then wake up and remember
*All of it . . . again*

# IN THE RELENTLESS HOUR

In the relentless hour
Of Time
Ticking away . . .
Think not of minutes
Think beyond the moment
To where
Time stands still.

Think of beauty born
In a moment
Whose indelible truth remains
Beyond the fact of living.
Think that centuries cannot
Destroy the living hour
Hold on to beauty
Grief is still a passing moment
Tears are only water
To revive
Nothing is lost
All pain has its reason
If only to remind us we are alive.

I was today and
I was also yesterday
And will be tomorrow
Beauty is all that matters
A child's smile
A friend
The trust that exists in the end
Between people of faith.

# FORGIVE ME

Forgive me if I do not cry
The day you die,
Streams at some seasons
Wind their way through country lanes of beauty
And are dry.

The willow bends its head
To kiss the empty river bed
With the same caress it gave
When in its heyday it was full and high
O river know that I remember
The splashing laughing clatter
Of a bubbling day in Spring
When everything was blossoming!

Butterflies still hover
Down the rocky bed
And weeds grow strong and
Guard the pebbled way.
In this high noon of nothing
Which is death
Brave flags still wave
Cowslip-parsley, rag weed and sorrel
Shout to me
That Spring is on her way
Comfort, I am still too deaf to hear.

Yet forgive me if I do not cry
The day you die

The simplest reason that I know
You said you'd rather have it so
And that I held my head serenely high
Remembering the love and glory that we knew.
Forgive me if I do not cry
The day you die.
Forgive me if once again
I do.

# THE LAST FAREWELL

SC  We must brace ourselves to the fact
     That we may never meet again.
     That the blood and tears that seal this pact
     Are not binding
     When in later years
     This world we know has turned to lead
     And among the trebled billions of the dead
     We wander through pits of fallen stars
     Searching each other
     And showing our hearts
     As token of our Love
     To the sightless eye of space.
     Let us now become aware
     That, as in this moment
     Of reality's sweet bliss,
     All seems unreal and we
     Not really here;
     So, in that blistering day of Truth,
     When among the lonely speechless stars
     We wander – bereft of these dear senses that
          we know –
     Unable to communicate –
     We may yet . . . be there. . .


WSC  But where?


180

*SC* Where indeed, along the note of this almighty
        theme
    Will the nightingale we know
    Find once again her first sung dream?
    In cavernous horrors of roaring red
    Will not our gentle dream be dead?
    O! Tell me once again of courage young
    And of the wise men dead from whom it
        sprung.

# VIII

# NEW POEMS

# BELLS

Sometimes I think my head is a chandelier
So many bells ring in it
I am as an open door
Ready for winds to play in it

Heather and blue bells
Honey and suckle
How can one keep one's head
Tie shoe or buckle?

When all of the heavens
Contrive to weave spells
To make one forget all
But blue sunlit bells . . .

# LONDON

All over the world
Aristocrats leave cities on Sunday –
I'm glad I am a peasant
For then my city
London
Belongs to me.

# NEVER LOOK BACK

Once more around
The Track
Bursting heart and mind
Only one goal
The end in mind –
Never look back.

# FOR SYLVIA HENLEY*

*'Who is Sylvia,*
*What is she?*
*That everyone adores her?'*
*She is Sylvia of the Seven Seas.*

When the turmoil of the long day's calm,
And all that anyone can do,
Seems not to soothe the troubled breast
She's Sylvia at her patient best

She's Sylvia on a tranquil night
There to appreciate the silver light
Of some unknown endeavour

She's Sylvia in a storm
That rips the roof off
So many hearts' most cherished dreams . . .

She's Sylvia of a thousand things of detail
Yet the whole design does not escape
Or daunt her tapestry.

She's Sylvia of a thousand schemes
Of putting everything and everyone together

She's Sylvia of the Seven Seas and Stormy Weather
She's Sylvia of compassion
Who sees the world's disorder
But wearilessly turns
And threads her needle once again for
The glory of it all.

188

She's Sylvia without end
She is my cheer leader
When my heart begins to pall

*She is Sylvia —*
*And my friend.*

# FOR THOSE WHO LOVE THE SUNLIGHT

I wouldn't care if it were night for me
But for those who love the sunlight
I will strive to be
And put myself into the game of life
And be a pawn
Of death
Or life

There is no passive hour here
Even the oak wood creaks
Hearing no longer the remnants
Of the tree it sprang from.

# FOR JULIA LOCKWOOD

The children in the garden have all grown up
No ripples stir the jade green pool
The calls, the shouts: *'Is Julie there?'*
Hang in the memory of the silent air.

The helicopter flies above
But 'Peter' isn't there
Don't be sad —
Don't look back
There's only winter here
But Spring is always with you
When you care,
As you can care . . .

Ahead, ahead lie
Unknown lands, and thoughts
And dreams, and people too
And from so many million
People
Remember
Some day, you'll find you.

# SUMMER HOLIDAY, ITALY, 1971

Is it the heat that makes me so listless?
Or is it my heart?
Why do I want to sit
Less
With people
And find backstreets – with door
Or is it my heartbeat
Or is it that burning, eating sun
That eats us up
While we bask and crawl back from the sea shore
Dizzy and skinless
And ask for more
"Oh, we are forever done!"

Wicked and contemptuous sun
All creatures crawl
Toward your light
You burn the toes of my dog's paw
As he strides bravely over the boiling sand
And a new found feller only four
Plods wearilessly if querulously
Over hot tar –
'Baah' – he says.
And 'pow' – too, I says!

I'll find a mountain top of snow,
In which small feet and paws can tread,
And we can drown you wicked summer sun
Only to learn
The ice has fire
And now frostbite
"Oh – we are forever done!"

# THE MASK

Behind the pallid mask
We call the face
The heart can sink or rise
The gentlest hope
The wildest thought
Can race the pulse
Or tear the entrails wide

Yet all the turmoil
That a heart can know
Can ebb before it reach the eyes
Can storm in vain across the smile
That steals across the well-schooled face
That wisely learns its task
And shielding well the foolish heart
No answers make
No reason ask.

# SO THIS IS HOW IT ENDS?

After all the passion
The tears, the smart
The questioning of self
The lee-way and the head-way
The hope that once again
There might be love
We have to part

And where now?
I see a silver sea
I hear music
And my heart
Still beats

The streets
Still stand awaiting
Passively forlorn
Despite the noise of traffic.
And I?
I sit within the shell of my house
And await some other dawn.

# IX

# SONGS BY

# SOME OF MY FRIENDS

# ANTHONY MONTAGUE BROWNE

## DIMINUENDO

Complying with convention, let us hand
In the full panoply of outraged pride.
Banish the whimper, let it be a bang!
For he, or she, has blundered – no, has lied!

Let us therefore end as God intended
As we cannot possess all, seek therefore none
And since it seems perfection is offended,
Cast out in one what we so slowly won?

But I to miserliness would rather hold,
With peasant greed eke out the little store,
And slowly ascending to the scaffold
Delay and pretext each lost rung the more.

*– 1943*

# MARY SPENCER CHURCHILL

# SONG

To some this world is grey and cold,
Life's way for them is crossed by fears,
And shrouded in a mist of tears.
To me, life's full of joys and gold,
My hopes gleam in the light of youth,
Undimmed by sorrows, free from cares.
But God to each in justice shares
Burdens and joys; and for a youth
Of happiness like mine, will give
A fight to fight, a pain to bear.
And earnestly I make this prayer
That though in sorrow I may live,
I never may forget this truth –
That I was happy in my youth.

*– 1939*

# VILLIERS DAVID

## SONNET

Celestial ruse, the moon lies in my glass
a trembling giant by my cocktail fondled,
a fleeting captive till my fingers close
around my challenger; then hiding, handled.
Shall I not drink the thimbleful of gin
And gulp the moon down, while its beauty draws
Music and fire, and begs my lips to sing
" . . . *with cinnamon sail and orchid oars* . . . "?

O double ruse, no moon lies in my glass
the marvel at its heart, though, mine entwines
For lovers, look behind the dreamers' fence
That brightness in the shade, that white, white rose
*They* have secured, those dear, those lawless Twins—
My own dear yes, my only passionate friends.

# PATRICK DESMOND

## YESTERDAY I WENT TO A FUNERAL

O Man
Who created God in thine own image
And built a Church in which to imprison Him
O Man
Who knoweth the way to the moon
And a quicker way to thine own destruction
O Man
Who hath power to do great good
And doth great evil
Please, Man
Teach us a better way to say goodbye
To fellow creatures when they die
Than in a bleak clinically clean chapel
With a poor puppet of a parson
Mouthing indistinctly blasphemous insincerities
And dreary hymns which no one really knows –
If a public performance there must be
Let it have light, love
And why not laughter
And a real cremation?
Not discreetly drawn curtains
Revealing unseemly thoughts
*Is* the costly coffin burnt?

*O Man*
*Put Aside Priorities*
*Just get the last rites right.*

# CHARLES HAMBLETT

## PROEM

In me a dozen devils wreak their devilry
And heart knocks love and hate with every beat,
Fingers of thorn tug at the rooted mystery
And kisses burn like stars where thunders meet;
    And many-fisted candles feed the flame
    Of this wild love no knocking heart can tame.

## JULIA LOCKWOOD

## THE WATCH

I gaze upon you sleeping there –
And wonder how we two shall fare!
Two creatures of this tempted world,
This rocky earth, that once was hurled
By giant hands, with strength and care
And placed us all together there!

You sleep in peace – no puckered brow!
What thoughts do *you* have – darling, now?
Oh! shall I wake you, kiss your eyes
Or shall I glance to heaven's skies,
And ask *Him* how we two shall fare
While you lie innocent, sleeping there?

# HAL SHAPER

## PRINCE OF LIARS

I have seen the majesty of truth
And would still rather be a Prince of Liars
A maker of magic carpets
Or a beggar in search of Samarkand
For while I search
I can make the stars sing songs that no one ever heard
And on that carpet fly my life through avenues of hope
Down streets of dreams,
And always towards some bright tomorrow.

I can find more stories in a sea-shell
Than the sea can find in an ocean
More magic in a moonbeam
Than the moon can find in the sky
And more songs in the garden of my imagination
Than the winds have sung in the wilderness of reality
I can still find more embroidery in an incident
Than any Flemish weaver in a tapestry.

The truth is finally just that –
But a Prince of Liars
Will still see diamonds in the damaged eyes of
    lonely people
Still see pearls in the tears of the dying
And still in the sanity of living
See the Glorious Madness of it all.

# LOBO NOCHO

## SHOW BIZ

What a life on the stage
Director's always in a rage,
Long rehearsals every day
Then at night you do the play.

Loads of make-up on the face
Backstage is a real cold place,
Dancers limber in the hall
Then you hear the half-hour call.

Lights out front start to dim,
Watch your step – the cat-walk's thin.
Musicians tune up in the pit,
Front rows' where the critics sit.

Overture is played real loud
Tonight it is a noisy crowd.

When the curtain starts to rise
You are nervous with the hives,
Remember now what you should do
Make damned sure you get that cue.

Fifteen minutes between two acts,
No time even to have a snack
Back on stage the second half
Hope the people have a laugh.
If you get a curtain call
Then you know they've had a ball.

Twice a week, a matinee,
Union dues we all must pay.
Booking agent, ten per cent
You're not broke – just slightly bent.

(*Sometimes you must wear a wig
If you want to keep a gig*)

Show's a hit, a nice long run.
Show Biz is Work
And lots of fun!

# LESLIE FREWIN

## CHURCHYARD: AFTER MATINS

There is only silence
In the arthritic shaft shadows
Of fleshless lives long past
Grass and weed and moss on faint dismembered
    stone
Of a hillock wet with old tears
A dull memory
Of some jubilant forgotten youth.
Nothing stirs, neither corpuscles or tender's bill
Still is the touch of a hand,
Cold the sight of a sigh
Unheard the bird
On mossy Gothic cill
Store of the whore of remembered times:
Only the cracked echo
Chimes

Not a branch stirs
No reeds of Bach weep
In the tumbril of vergers' time
A scudding cloud does not break the pattern
Of the distant coloured panes
Of old enmities.
Ensemble of effigious images
Remains inert:
Nothing reveals
The loneliness of nothing

Thoughts are still
A crow's look, a starling's stare
There
Threatens to turn a leaf

(A latent joy!)
Bare to its crone veins –
The Norman tower
Remains unacknowledged
As does the hour.

## ALEC WILDER

## ON VIEWING A DRAWING OF SELF

Thank you for a face I never had
Not because I'd like to have had it
But because it warms me to see
The decency I tried for:
All that striving to be
As affirmative as a tree,
As passive as a flower,
As dignified in defeat as a wolf,
As constant as a parent bird,
As orderly as the tide.
How could you know,
In the tangle of my failures,
That I always made a point of goodness
Since error, seldom trial
Shows in the eyes of a striver?
Yet you sensed, beneath the tempest,
A worshiper of life as it could be.
I humbly thank you.

# The Contributors to
## *Songs By Some of My Friends*

ANTHONY MONTAGUE BROWNE was for sixteen years the invaluable and trusted aide to Sir Winston Churchill. *Diminuendo* is his first published poem.

MARY SPENCER CHURCHILL, sister of Sarah, is the youngest daughter of Sir Winston Churchill. She is married to Sir Christopher Soames. *Song* is her first published poem.

VILLIERS DAVID is a writer and painter. He is the author of several books including the novel *Love In London,* and *Advice To My Godchildren*. His paintings have had exhibitions at the Wildenstein, Hazlitt and other galleries. *Sonnet* is his first published poem.

PATRICK DESMOND was for many years producer of the annual stage presentation of J. M. Barrie's *Peter Pan* – he produced Sarah Churchill in the title role, and in other plays. *Yesterday I Went To A Funeral*, is his first published poem.

CHARLES HAMBLETT is the author of a number of books including *Who Killed Marilyn Monroe?* and a biography of Marlon Brando. He was co-author (with Jane Deverson) of *Generation X*. He has published several volumes of poetry and edited the war anthology, *I Burn For England*.

JULIA LOCKWOOD is the actress daughter of Margaret Lockwood. She played Wendy to Sarah Churchill's *Peter Pan* in 1958 and a year later herself played the title role in the Barrie fantasy. *The Watch* is her first published poem.

LOBO NOCHO is an international actor, singer, musician and painter who lives in New York. His paintings are hung in many private collections. As an actor, he has featured in many films and appeared as The Devil in John Huston's *The Bible. Show Biz* is his first published poem.

HAL SHAPER is the lyricist of countless songs including *Softly, As I Leave You*, many of which have been recorded by Frank Sinatra, Barbra Streisand and other artistes. *The Prince of Liars* is his first published poem.

ALEC WILDER is an American classical and popular composer and arranger. He has arranged music for countless top artists and orchestras including Sinatra, Peggy Lee, Mildred Bailey, Dorsey, Goodman, Red Norvo and others. Among his compositions are *I'll Be Around. On Viewing a Drawing Of Self* was written specially for this volume.

LESLIE FREWIN is both author and publisher. He has published hundreds of authors, and has himself written eighteen books including *Dietrich*, an American Literary Guild Choice. His prize-winning short story, *The End of Summer*, represents British short story writing in the California State University's Freshman Reader, *Reading For Insight.*

212

# LIST OF TITLES

# INDEX OF FIRST LINES

# LIST OF TITLES

# INDEX OF FIRST LINES

214